TRAINS IN EUROPE IN THE 1970s

DAVID REED

To Sarah and Joe, who both enjoy travelling

First published 2024

Amberley Publishing
The Hill, Stroud
Gloucestershire, GL5 4EP

www.amberley-books.com

Copyright © David Reed, 2024

The right of David Reed to be identified as the Author of this work has been asserted in accordance with the Copyrights, Designs and Patents Act 1988.

ISBN 978 1 3981 1817 1 (print)
ISBN 978 1 3981 1818 8 (ebook)

All rights reserved. No part of this book may be reprinted or reproduced or utilised in any form or by any electronic, mechanical or other means, now known or hereafter invented, including photocopying and recording, or in any information storage or retrieval system, without the permission in writing from the Publishers.

British Library Cataloguing in Publication Data.
A catalogue record for this book is available from the British Library.

Typesetting by SJmagic DESIGN SERVICES, India.
Printed in the UK.

Introduction

Following on from my three previous railway books, *Steam Railways*, *Diesel and Electric Trains* and *Trains in the Southern Region in the late 1960s and early 1970s*, this book explores my early 1970s trips to visit the railways of Europe. I saw some of the last steam and vintage electric traction together with contemporary diesel and electric locomotives.

My visit to France took place in late November 1970 by train and Sealink ferry. We saw the last of the SNCF Class 141R 2-8-2 steam locomotives at Boulogne and Calais, returning by Seaspeed hovercraft.

In March 1972 I was fortunate enough to visit Portugal on the Locomotive Club of Great Britain's 'Douro' rail tour. In addition to two wonderful steam-hauled rail tours on the broad- and narrow-gauge lines of the Douro Valley, we flew there and back in a Monarch Airlines Bristol Britannia turboprop aircraft.

My journey to Austria was from Victoria via Dover Marine, now Western Docks, and Ostend by train and ship and took in the narrow-gauge railways of upper Austria as well as standard-gauge lines. The trains we used were steam, electric and diesel hauled. We saw and travelled behind several quite old electric locomotives dating back to the 1920s.

A couple of trips were made to Switzerland in 1974 by train and ship and were almost exclusively hauled by electric locomotives. A winter trip was made in February via Liverpool Street, Harwich and the Hook of Holland, and a summer journey in July from Waterloo via Weymouth Quay and Cherbourg.

In the 1970s there were none of today's budget airlines; Freddie Laker's Laker Airways had only just started operating in 1966. The Channel Tunnel was just a pipe dream, so most trips to Europe were still made in the classic manner: by train and cross-Channel ferry or hovercraft.

I count myself fortunate that I was able to experience European rail travel at such an interesting time and with such a variety of locomotives and trains. The Portuguese Douro Valley line in particular has changed with the building of five dams and associated locks, and consequent rise in water level. The railways in all the countries featured now have modern traction. Some routes have closed and others have been modernised. Any steam trains remaining are operated on a heritage or tourist basis, some over much-reduced distances.

When I started work in the early 1970s I was able to afford my first 35mm SLR camera, a basic Zenith, with which I took the photographs in this book. My photographic records are very much in the way of 'souvenir' pictures illustrating the various trips, taken from public viewpoints and with no special access arrangements. The pictures were all taken by me and none have been published previously. I made only the very briefest of notes at the time, so I have had to rely on these, augmented by reference to books and magazines. I apologise for any caption errors that may have arisen as a result.

I thank my wife, Margaret, for her support during the preparation of this book, and my friend of many years John Dawson, who arranged the two trips to Switzerland. My thanks are also due to Amberley for publishing this, my fourth book.

With my brother, Roger, and some friends I made a day trip to Boulogne and Calais on a dank and misty 28 November 1970 to see the last of the French National Railways (SNCF) steam locomotives. Baldwin-built 2-8-2 loco No. 141 R 576 and another Class 141R are seen here on shed at Boulogne.

No. 050524 and another 0-10-0 tank loco, with connecting rods removed and stowed on the tank tops, await their last journeys on 28 November 1970. This wheel arrangement is known as 'Decapod', after crustaceans with ten legs.

A massive 151T or 2-10-2 tank loco, No. 151 TQ 10, is cold at Boulogne shed in the company of some 141Rs, also on 28 November 1970.

On the same date 2-8-2 Class 141R No. 141 R 476, built by the Baldwin Locomotive Works of America, simmers at Boulogne shed.

The front of No. 141 R 511, also at Boulogne, has been cleaned and brightened up with a fresh coat of red paint applied to the buffer beam.

A couple of 141R 2-8-2 locos, Nos 141 R 511 and 141 R 476, are seen on shed at Boulogne on 28 November 1970. The nearest, No. 141 R 476, is in light steam.

Here is a frontal portrait of No. 141 R 511, built by Baldwin. These locos were supplied by United States and Canadian builders under the terms of the Lend-Lease plan during the Second World War. They were used all over the SNCF network from 1945 until the 1970s. The locos were built by companies such as Baldwin, Lima and Montreal Locomotive Works, with later batches being supplied as oil burners.

No. 141 R 48 was built by Lima Locomotive Works and had been receiving attention to its smokebox.

Another view of No. 141 R 511 at Boulogne on 28 November 1970.

We were hauled from Boulogne to Calais by CC 72022, seen here on 28 November 1970. Ninety of these 3,550 hp diesel-electric locos were built by Alstom-SACM from 1967. As SNCF pursued its policy of electrification the locos were moved around the country.

No. 040 D 16 is an 0-8-0 tender loco, which sits despondently at Calais on 28 November 1970.

A time exposure shows a desolate view of a sad end for No. 040 D 454. The 0-8-0 tender loco is out of steam at Calais as it sits reflected in a puddle awaiting its fate.

I participated in the Locomotive Club of Great Britain 'Douro' rail tour from Porto up the Douro Valley and back on 18 March 1972. Here is Caminhos de Ferro Portugueses, now Comboios de Portugal or Portuguese National Railways (CP) No. 295, all polished up and ready to depart from São Bento station, Porto, with the special tour train.

A CP Class 1400 diesel loco, built in 1967 by English Electric, passes with a service to Porto São Bento. These locos are still in service in 2023, with at least one in this blue livery.

Oil-fired Henschel No. CP295 of 1913 makes a photographic run-past for the benefit of the rail tour participants. The line was built to the 5-foot 6-inch broad gauge, or Iberian gauge, and opened in 1887. It runs up the Douro Valley for 109 miles through the heart of the port wine region.

En route we saw 2-8-0 No. 714, also oil-fired, doing a spot of shunting. The loco was built by the North British Locomotive Company around 1910 to 1920.

Another Mallet 2-4-0+0-6-0 tank loco is seen on a mixed train, believed to be at Ermesinde, junction for the narrow-gauge line to Minho. Parcels are being unloaded from broad-gauge vans on the adjacent track.

Inside-cylindered 4-6-0 No. CP284, rather reminiscent of the Holden B12 Class of the Great Eastern Railway, waits to back on to the tour train at Regua. The port wine transit shed behind the locomotive is now a restaurant.

No. CP284, built by Henschel in 1910, is seen during one of several photo stops. The tour train was comprised of first- and second-class carriages sandwiching a Wagons-Lits restaurant car, the height of luxury.

A mixed passenger and van train heading up the valley from Ferradosa is seen crossing the old viaduct over the Douro River. In the mid- to later 1970s dams were built across the river and some bridges rebuilt, which has resulted in almost submerging the piers but leaving the lattice girders above water.

Henschel 4-6-0 No. CP284 is seen again, believed to be at Pocinho station.

An outside cylinder Henschel 4-6-0 No. CP211 dwarfs a small tank engine at Pocinho.

Inside-cylindered No. CP281 of 1910 is pictured with No. CP211 in the background at Pocinho.

The tour train hauled by No. CP284 is looped at Pocinho. This was in order to pass an 0400 series diesel railcar dating from the mid-1960s and heading back towards Porto.

No. CP284 is turned ready for the return journey on the turntable at Barca d'Alva. Although the line from Pinhão to Barca d'Alva and Salamanca is closed, the distinctive three-track loco shed at Barca d'Alva is still standing in 2023.

Prior to the return journey to Porto, Henschel 4-6-0 No. CP284 takes water at Barca d'Alva.

Spanish National Railways (RENFE) Class 303 Sulzer-engined 0-6-0 diesel locomotive No. 10332 shunts on the border between Portugal and Spain at Barca d'Alva. The Spanish line from Salamanca closed in 1985 and the Portuguese line between Pinhão and Barca d'Alva closed in 1988.

No. E41, a diminutive short wheelbase 0-6-0 tank engine, on shed at Regua.

Waiting on shed at Regua is 2-6-4 tank loco No. CP075.

Pristine 4-6-0 No. CP295, which had hauled us from Porto earlier, and somewhat dirtier 2-6-4 tank loco No. CP076 are berthed around the turntable at Regua. The turntable is still in place in 2023.

The tour train is seen here at Regua, now hauled by No. CP0184, a Henschel 2-8-4 tank loco built in 1924. No. CP0186 of this class is now preserved and hauls a 'Historic Train' between Regua and Pocinho.

In the evening of 18 March 1972, a time exposure captures No. CP0184 simmering on arrival back at Porto São Bento station.

The following day, a very damp 19 March 1972, a narrow-gauge tour train was provided for the LCGB group for a tour of the area's narrow-gauge lines. The train, hauled by Henschel 2-8-2 tank No. E142, is seen here posing at a photo stop.

En route, this elderly 2-6-0 tank loco No. CP/E83, built by Emil Kessler in 1886, was observed taking on water. The 'E' prefix denotes narrow gauge, from the Portuguese *estreita*, meaning narrow.

Henschel 2-8-2 tank No. E142, heading the tour train, performs a dramatic photographic run-past on the viaduct over the Ave River at Vila do Conde. No. E142 was built in 1931.

The 2-8-2 tank, No. E142, and tour train provides another photographic run-past at Póvoa de Varzim. This station was closed in 2002 and now the modern electric Porto Metro runs here.

An 0-4-0+0-4-0 Mallet tank loco No. CP/E170, built by Henschel in the early 1900s, with 2-8-2T No. E141 in the background, is seen at Lousado.

At Lousado station, CP/E167, built by Henschel in the 1900s, has now taken over the tour train and pauses for a photographic stop.

CP/E167 is seen here taking on water.

At Paçô Vieira, No. CP/E167 leans to the curve as it waits for a train to pass in the opposite direction. Tour participants seize the opportunity to view the loco and take photographs.

While the tour train pauses at Paçô Vieira an elderly diesel railcar passes. Built by Allan of Rotterdam in the mid-1950s, these railcars were completely modernised in 2000.

During another pause for photographic purposes at Fafe, northern terminus, the driver is seen reboarding No. CP/E167.

The final locomotive change was to provide 2-6-0 tank loco No. CP/E102, built by Emil Kessler in the early 1900s. It is seen here during a photo stop between Maia and Araujo.

Some local children are intrigued by the interest shown in No. CP/E102 by the tour participants.

All cameras to the fore as we pass another steam-hauled train headed by Henschel No. CP/E211, a 2-4-0+0-6-0 Mallet tank loco built in the early 1920s.

It is journey's end at Porto Trindade station and an exchange of views is taking place between the train crew.

At Porto Trindade on 19 March 1972, No. CP/E102 and the tour train are seen alongside a rather dirty Allan of Rotterdam diesel unit.

Also at Porto Trindade, this blue Allan of Rotterdam diesel unit, built in the 1950s, is somewhat cleaner.

An 0-6-0 tank loco of the E51 class, built by Emil Kessler in 1889, has seen better days and now provides a handy and weatherproof support for a line of washing. It is in the company of a railcar truck, No. ME21, converted from a lorry for the CP in 1944.

En route to Austria later in 1972, a Class 22 electric locomotive of Belgian National Railways (SNCB), No. 2214, built in the mid-1950s, is pictured with a baggage car at Ostend on 21 June.

The following day, 22 June 1972, nearly new Austrian Federal Railways (ÖBB) Class 1042 No. 1042.537, in new red livery, is seen at Linz. These locos operated on 15 kV AC and 197 were built between 1967 and 1977. These were the first ÖBB locos to be painted in this red livery.

We travelled on some of the Stern & Hafferl lines in Upper Austria. These lines used a variety of railcars and former tramcars, many dating from the 1930s or earlier. On 22 June 1972 a very clean four-wheeler or Bo No. ET22.104, built in 1912, is seen here at Linz Lokalbahnhof.

An elderly Bo-Bo steeple-cab loco built around 1916, No. E20.005, is seen here coupled to No. ET22.104 and with a trailer coach in tow, also on 22 June 1972.

An ÖBB Class 2045 standard-gauge centre-cab Bo-Bo diesel loco, built in the early 1950s, is seen making its way through a wooded valley on a local train comprised of open-balcony four-wheeled carriages on 22 June 1972.

Class 52 No. 52 7597, built in 1944, fitted with a caboose tender, hauls a freight train near Lungitz on 22 June 1972.

We walked to St Georgen where another Class 52, No. 52 7017, built in 1943 and here fitted with a Giesl oblong ejector, is also seen heading a freight train on the same date in June 1972.

The following morning, 23 June 1972, Class 52 No. 52 7405 of 1943 is pictured at Lungitz. These were the equivalent of the German Class 50 'Kreigslok' austerity locos, also built during the Second World War.

On 23 June 1972, Stern & Hafferl Bo tram No. ET24.101 built in 1931, is pictured at Lambach prior to a run down to Gmunden.

At Vorchdorf on the same date in June 1972 an elderly Stern & Hafferl tram, built in 1936, has stopped to serve a couple of the local populace.

With the Traunsee lake in the background, a trio of ÖBB four-wheeled railcars are pictured at Gmunden awaiting custom on the evening of 23 June 1972. These Class 5081 lightweight diesel-mechanical vehicles were built in the mid-1960s.

At Garsten, on 24 June 1972 we saw ÖBB Class 0298 No. 298.52, built by Krauss in 1898, being made ready for service. At this time Garsten was the junction between the ÖBB standard- and narrow-gauge lines.

Class 0298 No. 298.53 is about to depart with the 11.58 train on 24 June 1972. It will run down the valley of the Steyr River from Garsten via Grünburg and Mölln to Klaus. The northern section of the route between Steyr and Grünburg is now operated as the Steyrtalbahn heritage railway.

No. 298.53, also dating from 1898, takes on water at Mölln by means of a rather Heath Robinson-style water crane.

At Mölln station No. 298.53 is pictured with a local train of elderly open-balcony four-wheeled carriages and a van.

This is one of many venerable electric locomotives we saw in Austria. No. 1073.20, a jackshaft-driven 1-C-1 of the early 1920s, is pictured with a train of four-wheeled carriages at Garsten on the evening of 24 June 1972.

Also pictured at Garsten on the same June evening is an elderly ÖBB Class 1018 1-Do-1 electric loco of 1940 in the new bright red livery but hauling some old four-wheeled carriages.

In typical ÖBB style, a steam locomotive chassis has been converted into a snow plough, No. 985.21. It is seen in a quiet siding at Linz shed awaiting the winter months.

Pictured at rest on shed at Linz is Class 52 2-10-0 No. 52.7405. The Class 52 was a simplified version of the German Class 50, aimed at reducing construction time and cutting down on scarce materials. Thousands of these locos were built during the war. Note the guard's cabin built into the tender.

ÖBB Class 50 2-10-0 loco No. 50.685 at Linz shed. Built in 1940 to a Deutsche Reichsbahn (DR) Second World War design, many were left in other countries after the war, such as this example in Austria. No. 50.685 is now preserved in Germany.

The old, the very old and the not so old lined up at Linz! Class 52 No. 52.7405 is seen again in the company of a veteran electric loco, No. 1080.17, built in the mid-1920s, and a more modern Bo-Bo electric loco, No. 1041.09, dating from the 1950s.

Pictured at Ebelsberg on 25 June 1972, the tram from Linz (in white) connects with the Stern & Hafferl Lokalbahn railcar from Ebelsberg to St Florian. The St Florian branch closed in 1973 and is now operated as a museum line.

The 126-year-old Pöstlingbergerbahn is a metre-gauge railway linking Linz with the Pöstlingberg mountain outside the city. Seen here on 25 June 1972, a railcar enters the summit citadel station having climbed 255 metres in 4 km. Between 2008 and 2009 the Pöstlingbergerbahn was modernised, re-gauged and integrated with the Linz trams.

A Stern & Hafferl railcar built around 1912, with two trailer vehicles in tow, arrives at the Linz Lokalbahnhof at 08.43 on 26 June 1972.

The DB Class 103 electric locos were introduced from the early 1970s, so this one was very new when photographed leaving Linz on 26 June 1972. In its distinctive red and white livery, it was heading the 'Prinz Eugen' Trans Europe Express (TEE) service introduced in 1971 between Vienna and Bremen.

By contrast an old ÖBB Class 1018 built around 1939, No. 1018.03, waits at Linz on 26 June 1972 while some passengers board.

Another elderly ÖBB electric loco, 1045.08, with similarly elderly four-wheeled carriages in tow, awaits departure from the terminus station at Kammer-Schörfling on the shore of the Attersee lake on 26 June 1972.

Across the lake, a Stern & Hafferl railcar and trailer await departure with the next service from Attersee to Vöcklamarkt on 26 June 1972.

At Vöcklamarkt, a mixed train on the Atterseebahn connects with the ÖBB main line. Passengers board the 12.20 departure to Attersee on 26 June 1972.

A hot steam locomotive contrasts with the 'Eskimo' ice cream advertisement on what I remember to be a very hot day at Vöcklamarkt. Class 52 No. 52.1337, with guard's cabin tender, awaits departure.

Two 2-10-0s await their next duties. Among the subtle differences, the nearest has a Geisel ejector and solid disc pony truck wheel while the furthest has a conventional chimney and spoked pony wheel.

With its power vehicle towards the camera, an ÖBB 'Transalpin' set, No. 4010.02, heads away from Linz on 27 June 1972.

A 5046 series diesel hydraulic railcar together with a trailer and two other additional carriages calls at Wieselburg on 27 June 1972.

Arriving at Ober-Grafendorf on 27 June 1972 is a Class 2091 type 1-Bo-1 narrow-gauge diesel loco built in 1936, together with two four-wheeled carriages. The loco is in the latest ÖBB red livery.

On 27 June 1972, narrow-gauge C-C electric locomotive No. 1099.02, built in 1909, arrives at Ober-Grafendorf on the only ÖBB narrow-gauge electrified line, between St Pölten and Mariazell. In the 1960s these locos were rebodied. Drive to the three axles on each bogie is by jackshafts and rods.

At St Pölten on 27 June 1972, a modern Class 4010 'Transalpin' set No. 4010.03 on the left, built in 1965, compares with a more elderly Class 4030 No. 4030.20 dating from the mid-1950s.

Trains in Europe in the 1970s

A Class 2050 Bo-Bo diesel-electric loco, No. 2050.17, built around 1958, enters Tulln on a service for Gmünd on 27 June 1972. A number of elderly carriages are in tow and plenty of custom is on offer.

From across the border, a then new East German Deutches Reichsbahn (DR) high-speed 100 mph diesel train, No. 175 007-4, arrives at Gmünd on the 'Vindobona' service. Like the British Inter-City 125 HST, there is a driving motor vehicle at each end, but with only three intermediate trailer cars.

ÖBB Class 93 2-8-2 tank loco No. 93.1320 shunts in the goods yard at Gmünd on 28 June 1972.

A Czechoslovakian Railways (CSD) 2-10-0 No. 534.0331, with a large red star emblazoned on its smokebox door, arrives across the border at Gmünd on 28 June 1972.

ÖBB Class 399 narrow-gauge loco No. 399.05 arrives at Gmünd with a freight from the Gross Gerungs line. Note the standard-gauge wagons loaded on narrow-gauge transporter wagons.

With a train of elderly four-wheeled open-balcony carriages, No. 93.411, fitted with a Geisel ejector, calls at Schwarzenau on 28 June 1972.

Class 93 2-8-2T pauses at Zwettl prior to returning to Schwarzenau on 28 June 1972.

The old and the new in contrast on the evening of 28 June 1972. Another DR streamlined diesel train catches the setting sun as it accelerates past an ÖBB Class 93 steam loco shunting freight wagons at Schwarzenau.

Class 399 No. 399.01 is seen pristine in ex-works condition at Gmünd on 29 June 1972. These locos were of the unusual 0-6-4 wheel arrangement, having an articulated tender.

A Czechoslovakian Class 556 2-10-0 locomotive, No. 556.015, crosses the Czech border into Austria at Gmünd on 30 June 1972.

On 30 June 1972, ÖBB Class 399 No. 399.05 is ready to leave Gmünd on a freight train including a standard-gauge wagon on a narrow-gauge transporter. The leading coach was provided for the use of railway shunting and other staff in the goods yards along the route.

Class 2095 narrow-gauge diesel loco No. 2095.12 leaves Gmünd with a mixed passenger and van train on 30 June.

Class 93 No. 93.1390 is seen on shed at Gmünd on 30 June.

Raabs station was the end of the now closed line from the junction at Göpfritz. Class 93 No. 93.1427 is seen waiting in the rain with two elderly four-wheeled carriages on 30 June 1972.

A trio of elderly ÖBB Class 1072 jackshaft- and rod-driven 1-Bo-1 electric locomotives, built in 1913 and headed by No. 1072.08, stand awaiting their next duties at Vienna Nord depot on 1 July 1972.

One of the magnificent Class 78 4-6-4 'Baltic' tank locos, No. 78.616, is seen inside the shed at Vienna Nord depot on 1 July.

Undergoing maintenance at Vienna Nord is a Class 5041 railcar. Built in 1933, the vehicle seated sixty-four passengers. A couple of wheelsets await fitting in the foreground, one powered and the other non-powered.

A Class 77 4-6-2 'Pacific' tank loco, No. 77.25, awaits departure from Praterstern station, Vienna, on the 16.20 late afternoon service to Retz. We caught this 1 July service with its train of elderly four-wheeled open-balcony carriages.

Having shown interest in the loco, we were invited by the driver to take a cab ride on this impressive machine. I was spattered with oil from the air brake pump, but that was a small price to pay!

En route at Korneuburg we passed a Class 52 2-10-0 with guard's cabin tender on a freight train.

Our proud driver is momentarily distracted as he poses in front of his magnificent Class 77 loco at Retz on 1 July 1972.

In the evening light, 77.25 takes water at Hohenau en route back to Vienna on 1 July 1972.

Another view of No. 77.25 shunting at Retz after arrival with the 16.20 service from Vienna Paterstern on 1 July 1972.

Class 78 No. 78.613 poses at Vienna Praterstern station on 2 July 1972. Known since 1975 as Vienna Nord, this station is close to the Prater amusement park where the Great Wheel featured in the film *The Third Man* is located. No. 78.613 is making ready to depart with the 16.58 to Bernardsthal.

ÖBB Class 4030 EMU No. 4030.209 on a Schnellbahn suburban service arrives at Vienna Praterstern station.

Coupling, connecting rod, cylinder and air brake pump detail of 2-10-0 No. 52.3504 on shed at Stadlau on 3 July.

On the right, Class 93 No. 93.1326 waits with its train at Pirawarth while 93.1332 arrives from the Mistelbach direction on 3 July.

Class 1042 Bo-Bo electric loco No. 1042.507 in original green livery leaves Bruck an der Mur with the 14.51 express service to Graz and Spielfeld Strass on 4 July 1972.

ET11 is one of the 4042 series of single-car EMUs dating from 1936. This vehicle is serving the Steyrmarkt Landesbahnen privately owned line and is forming the 17.15 service from Peggau-Deutschfeistritz to Ubelbach.

A Jugoslav Railways (JZ) General Motors EMD series G16 diesel loco is seen at Spielfeld Strass on the then Yugoslav border with the 10.50 arrival, the 'Beograd Express' from Hamburg.

Trains in Europe in the 1970s

Jugoslav 2-8-2 steam loco No. 06.025, built by Borsig in 1930, leaves Spielfeld Strass on the 12.12 cross-border passenger service towards Zagreb.

En route to Graz we passed this 2-8-0 of the Graz Köflacher Bahn (GKB), formerly owned by the ÖBB, No. 56.3115. It was built around 1914 by WLF Floridsdorf and was doing a spot of shunting at Voitsberg on 5 July 1972.

Commonly known as 'Die Alte Dame' or 'The Old Lady', No. 671 of the GKB is pictured at Graz on 6 July 1972. A 2-6-2 tank loco, No. 30.114, built in 1900, is just visible behind. No. 671 is an 0-6-0 with double frames, and built in 1860, it is one of the longest-serving active steam locomotives.

GKB 2-8-0 No. 56.3249 shunts at Graz on 6 July 1972.

Pictured at Graz on 6 July 1972 is GKB 4-4-0 No. 406. This loco was built in 1896 for the Südbahn.

The ÖBB Eisenerz to Vordernberg standard-gauge rack railway was opened in 1891 to transport iron ore and provide a passenger service in what was a very remote area. Here, a Class 97-hauled passenger train is descending on 6 July 1972.

Through a torrential rainstorm on 6 July, two Class 97 rack locomotives expend great effort in lifting a train of iron ore to the summit of the line at Präbichl nearly 4,000 feet above sea level. The route includes gradients of up to 1 in 14.

As the mist and drizzle hang in the valley another heavy iron ore train is lifted up the gradient towards Präbichl on 6 July.

The view from my hotel bedroom window on 6 July as an empty train descends towards Eisenerz.

Our passenger train is propelled up the gradient into Vordernberg Markt by hard-working Class 97 No. 97.215 on 7 July 1972.

Headed by No. 97.205 with safety valves blowing, a loaded train arrives at the summit at Präbichl on 7 July. This line is now privately owned and operated as a heritage line.

Also on 7 July 1972, 0-6-2 tank loco No. 97.205, built in the 1890s in the works of the Vienna Locomotive Works, Floridsdorf, pauses between duties at the summit at Präbichl.

The calm after the day before! On 7 July 1972 a Class 5081 railbus waits at Vordernberg Markt, its exhaust drifting up vertically into the damp air. Some of these vehicles were specially modified for use on the steep gradients of the Vordernberg route.

ÖBB Class 1010 electric loco No. 1010.19 is pictured in green livery at Schwarzach-St Veit heading south towards the Tauern Tunnel on 7 July 1972.

Across the border, Italian Railways (FS) Class 668.1710 DMU heads from San Candido towards Brunico on 8 July 1972. These diesel hydraulic railcars were introduced from 1954 and improved over the years. This train was at the time very new, having been built in the early 1970s.

These Crosti-boilered Class 741 locomotives operated through the Puster Valley towards Brixen and were among the last of Italian steam locos. No. 741.320 is seen leaving San Candido with a freight train on 8 July 1972. Older, Class 743, locos had twin pre-heater barrels either side of the main boiler.

Class 741 No. 741.028 is shunting at San Candido on 8 July. These 2-8-0 locos, with a pre-heater boiler below the normal boiler and a side-mounted chimney, gave rise to the British Railways experiment to fit Crosti boilers to ten BR Class 9F 2-10-0s.

Trains in Europe in the 1970s 75

This picture shows 2-8-0 No. 741.189 leaving San Candido with the 18.31 mixed train into Italy on 8 July 1972. The absence of a conventional chimney on the smokebox gives a slightly unbalanced effect.

Another picture shows No. 741.189 heading away down the valley on the same occasion.

No. 741.028 is seen here banking the 18.31 service from San Candido shown previously.

These ÖBB 1A-Bo-A1, alternatively 2-8-2, electric locomotives were introduced in 1928. No. 1670.20 in the new red livery is arriving at Feldkirch with the 10.23 departure to Bregenz on 10 July 1972.

Class 2095 B-B diesel locos are the standard ÖBB narrow-gauge engines, built between 1958 and 1962. No. 2095.04 is waiting with the 12.12 departure from Bregenz to Bezau on 10 July. The Bersbuch to Bezau section now operates as the Walderbahnle tourist heritage line.

At Bregenz, No. 1020.43 is seen heading the 12.19 service to Bludenz on 10 July 1972. These locos were built between 1940 and 1944, originally for the DR, becoming Austrian stock after 1945. Besides local services, they were also used as pilot locos on trains over the Arlberg route.

Having crossed the border into Germany, German Federal Railways (DB) Class 220 No. 220.055 is pictured arriving at Lindau on 10 July 1972. These locos were built in the early 1950s by Krauss-Maffei and have hydraulic transmission. They became the basis of the BR Western Region Warship Class diesel hydraulic locos.

The DB Class 23 locomotives, of 2-6-2 wheel arrangement, were introduced after the Second World War to replace older life-expired locos. No. 023.055-2 is ready to depart on the 17.40 Ulm to Aachen service on 10 July 1972.

Two Class 52 2-10-0s, Nos 052 203-7 and 052 231-2, are seen between duties at Friedrichshafen on 10 July 1972.

Another DB Class 23, No. 023 012-8, is pictured on an early evening Ulm to Ludwigshafen service, on 10 July 1972.

En route to Switzerland, Nederlandse Spoorwegen (NS, Dutch Railways) MAT 54 'dog-nose' type electric multiple units were observed. Built for express services by Allan of Rotterdam in the mid-1950s, they can be of two cars, as shown here on 20 February 1974, or four cars and operate at 1,500 or 3,000 volts DC.

This picture shows NS 0-6-0 diesel-electric shunter No. 634, also on 20 February 1974. It is one of a class of sixty-five built in England by English Electric in the 1950s and has obvious design similarities with its British Railways cousins.

On 20 February 1974 a NS DE1 diesel multiple unit (DMU), commonly known as a 'blue angel', arrives at Arnhem.

A double vehicle electric locomotive, No. 118 52 of Swiss Federal Railways (SBB), is pictured at the Swiss Transport Museum in Luzerne in February 1974. Built in 1939 and with over 8,000 kW of power, it was the most powerful loco in the world. Following fire damage the loco was restored externally.

On view at the Swiss Transport Museum was standard-gauge Mallet 0-4-0+0-4-0 tank loco built by Maffei in 1893. Designed for freight operation, it worked until the late 1930s. It is pictured here in February 1974 and has since been restored to steam.

1-C-2 rod- and jackshaft-driven electric loco No. 10432 was also on display outside the Swiss Transport Museum but had not been preserved. It was built in 1925 and is also seen here in February 1974.

A Berner Oberland Bahn (BOB) train headed by ABeh 4/4 loco No. 305 operating at 1,500 volts DC is seen here at Wilderswil on 21 February 1974. Note the Riggenbach rack rails laid in the Schynige Platte track alongside to aid adhesion on the gradients on that line.

Preserved Jungfrau Bahn (JB) Class He 2/2 train dating from 1912 waits for passengers at Kleine Scheidegg in February 1974. This line uses the Strub rack system and the trains operate at 1,125 volts AC. The train has an open wagon attached for conveyance of skis.

The old and the new on the JB await passengers at Kleine Scheidegg. Jungfraujoch, the summit station, is the highest railway station in Europe. It reaches a level of over 3,400 metres and is around 500 metres below the actual Jungfrau mountain summit.

A JB train built around 1960 heads up the Jungfrau line. The line up to Jungfraujoch runs for 9 kilometres. It is partly in tunnel under the Eiger and Monch summits, and has a maximum gradient of around 1 in 4.

En route to Switzerland in July 1974, classic evening departures are lined up at Gare de Lyon. A BB16000 series 25 kV Bo-Bo electric loco is centre of the picture while on the right is a BB16500 series mixed-traffic electric loco. Both classes were built from 1958.

Also in July 1974, French National Railways (SNCF) BB16006 waits departure from Gare de Lyon with our night express to Berne.

Metre-gauge Class HG 3/3 tank locomotive No. 1068 is seen here on display at Interlaken. It was built in 1926 by SLM, the Swiss Locomotive & Machine works, for service on the Brünig Railway and was withdrawn in 1965. It has since been restored to operational use.

Berne-Löchtsberg-Simplon Railway (BLS) Class De 4/5 electric railcar No. 792 dating from 1929 waits at Interlaken in July 1974.

A view of the Schynige Platte Bahn in July 1974. This is a rack-operated line using the Riggenbach rack system and operates at 1,500 volts DC. The line is 7 kilometres in length, has a maximum gradient of 1 in 4, and reaches nearly 2,000 metres.

The Schynige Platte Bahn runs from Wilderswil station near Interlaken. It crosses the Breitlauenen Alp to the Schynige Platte, a mountain ridge with extensive views of lakes Brienz and Thun. The diminutive 0-4-0 locomotives date from 1910 and this photo was also taken in July 1974.

Bern-Lötchberg-Simplon Bahn (BLS) Class Re 4/4 arrives at Brig with a local service in July 1974. These locos were built by SLM and were introduced from 1964.

Swiss Federal Railways (SBB) Class Re 4/4 No. 11164, dating from 1964, enters Brig with an international train formed of SNCF coaching stock in July 1974.

Bo-Bo 'Crocodile' No. 11 of the Brig-Visp-Zermatt Railway (BVZ) is seen at Brig in July 1974. The line opened between Zermatt and Visp in 1891 and was extended to Brig in 1930, around the time the line was electrified. At Brig the BVZ connects with the Furka-Oberalp route.

The Furka-Oberalp Bahn (FOB) was established in the early 1920s. It runs via the Furka Pass, as seen here, from Brig to Andermatt and on to Disentis, where it connects with the Rhaetian Bahn (RhB).

Trains in Europe in the 1970s

In the heat of the July 1974 summer sun a SBB Re 4/4 Class locomotive arrives at Lugano on a service to Zürich and Basel.

A Class Ae 4/6, No. 10811, of 1-Bo-Bo-1 wheel arrangement is glimpsed at Bellinzona station in 1974. These powerful locos were built in 1941 for operation over the Gotthard route and feature flexible 'Java' bogies instead of the 1-Do-1 rigid chassis previously used in similar locos exported to Java.

The 'Metropolitano' express from Milan to Frankfurt is hauled by a SBB Class Re 4/4 loco as it whisks the train of Italian coaching stock through Brunnen in July 1974.

SBB Class Ce 6/8 articulated 'Crocodile' 1-C-C-1 passes through Brunnen with a freight train in July 1974. These locomotives were introduced in 1920 for freight haulage over mountain lines, especially the Gotthard route. They weigh 126 tons and are nearly 64 feet in length.

Also at Brunnen in July 1974, a Class Re 6/6 triple bogie Bo-Bo-Bo loco arrives. This loco is one of the first two built in 1972, having an articulated body, later locos having rigid bodies. The middle axles of these Bo-Bo-Bo locos give flexibility by being able to move sideways by up to 5 inches.

On the Rhaetian Railway (RhB) 'Baby Crocodile' No. 412 of C-C wheel arrangement and in its original brown livery has arrived at Davos. These locos were built in 1921 and the nose housings are mounted on the bogies. Each bogie is driven from its own motor via jackshafts and connecting rods.

In July 1974 RhB Class Ge 6/6 No. 705 arrives at Filisur, the first three coaches being filled by excited children. The locos date from around 1960, are of triple bogie Bo-Bo-Bo configuration and the bodies are articulated.

A RhB Class Ge 6/6 hauls its train across the Landwasser Viaduct near Filisur and straight into the tunnel. The viaduct, with its 200-foot-high pillars, was constructed in 1902 and has a radius of 300 feet. No scaffolding was used, each pillar being built up around a steel framework using cranes.

A RhB train formed of a Class ABe 4/4s near Alp Grüm station, with views towards the Palu glacier.

RhB Class ABDe 4/4 No. 483 waits at Chur in July 1974 prior to its run up to Arosa. Of Bo-Bo configuration, it was one of six built in the late 1950s.

Also in 1974, No. 487 of Class ABDe 4/4 makes its way through the streets of Chur on its way to Arosa.

The end of the journey and the end of this book. SBB Class Re 4/4 No. 10033 is seen in Trans Europe Express red and cream livery at Zürich after arrival with a mixed train in July 1974. The class dates back to 1946 and was designed to operate fast trains on easily graded routes.